MARBLE GODDESSES
WITH TECHNICOLOR SKINS

MARBLE GODDESSES
WITH TECHNICOLOR SKINS

Corinne Robins

SEGUE BOOKS
NEW YORK

For Sal and Joyce, most loved of artists

ISBN: 0-937804-84-3
Library of Congress Catalog Card No.: 00-102813

Cover art by Joyce Romano.

With special thanks to:
Joan Venum
Phyllis Kronick
James Sherry

Acknowledgments: *Ark/angel 2:*"The Beauty Thing"; *Another Chicago Magazine:* "Futurist Cookup," "Art Process"; *Caprice:* "Cut with a Kitchen Knife," "Agnes Thinking About God," "Venus-intra-Venus," "The Woman in the Ground," "From the Other Side of the Mirror," "Ready to Wear," "De Chirico's Afternoon Metaphysics," "Magic Show," "Frida's Feet," "Expressionism," "Figure on the Raised Bed," "The Guggenheim or Mr. Wright's House," "With his Eyes Closed;" *Confrontation:* "The Great Ladies," "The Sad Bearded Japanese Emperor," and "Mondrian"; *Hunger No.7:* "They Will Take My Island"; *M/e/a/n/i/n/g:* "Stella, the Star"; *Poetry, New York:* "In Caravaggio's Rooms" and "Figure on the Raised Bed" (revised).

Segue Books are distributed by
Small Press Distribution
1341 Seventh Avenue
Berkeley, CA. 94710-1403.
Phone orders: 800-869-7553
spdbooks.org

SEGUE BOOKS
are published by
The Segue Foundation
303 East 8th Street
New York, NY 10009
segue.org

CONTENTS

ARTISTS

IN CARAVAGGIO'S ROOMS

In a closet where he died —
my friend Paul was murdered by his lover
I read in the paper, walking where
the Caravaggios are hung; Caravaggio,
his pretty loves and murder done —
and only these pictures left to celebrate
how he lies with light, out of darkness
paints bowls of fruit beside painted cheeks,
setting Bible tales in robbers' dens.
Who did he touch? Painting mouths on mouths
of boys and saints, himself a fleshy rose, served up —

Three months ago: bar lights, Paul,
between us his voice rising,
talking fast over a nervous boy beside him;
his words overtopping overloaded plates,
leaving the hearer hungering after white leaded necks,
paths of rounded arms, peek-a-boo terror,
the boy squeezed, squeezed
under Paul's edgy anger and that voice
roping in childhood as a centerpiece
of soft white flesh—

Caravaggio, did you also walk
on the small bones of painted boys
once they were grown and no more beautiful?
Was it love or rage made you derange these bodies
into viola torsos, appeal to God
asking about violence, paint Saint Paul
as a man fallen below a horse—
who did he touch?—(in a church with candles

flickering as if God had forgiven him)
hoof shadows defining love
as bodies wrapped in chiaroscuro,
capering at the monster in the mirror
where desire—the hunt through shadowed night
is for forever?

MOVING HOUSES

Sitting in the silence of absences,
it is time to sell these rooms like years
with shadow furniture gone from oblong walls
as the light, always from the left,
sheds its silence on parquet cut
not unlike Vermeer's black and white
chess floors, girl and soldier
moving pieces, pictures sporting
tactile maps of unknown seas
in houses in which a table, a chair,
a glass and pitcher sit, the light
sliding, slipping that safety net
mooring the body —as tick goes the time clock,
and now it's sell, sell, sell —
my floor shifting under small table and piles
of floor plans in place of maps;
a house blown apart, footsteps on my heart
preserved in packed up objects,
in a bronze ballerina toe pointing out,
a lamp of childhood now become invisible,
in Northern winter light, in ships sailing
across the mind into the coolness
of empty rooms and that empty corner,
which once housed a vase on a Steinway piano —

It didn't break. It doesn't break
as shipwrecked behind half opened blinds,
waving across boundaries, through sunlight stripes,
I leave my past and enter small pictures to be safe
where Vermeer's couples bending over lutes
play at the game of time, the real estate of life,

amber music with sound a vanishing point,
someone somewhere singing while
the mind's *camera obscura* turns its back
on the bulk of my father's upright chair,
on personal memory (goodby, goodby!)
to enter into the fashions of an older modernity
where, by window light, a tipsy servant girl falls asleep
and pregnant women study love letters in quiet corners;
where a geographer displays his maps, close up and accurate,
and where using shadow through leaded glass,
close up and accurate, the painter constructs his universe.

THE FIGURE ON THE RAISED BED

".. she is a being at one with nature in a fleshly simplicity that,
he insists, is the most abominable of artifices."
                              Angela Carter, BLACK VENUS

Does she signal the end of seduction?
Yes, yes! "Lie back, lie back"
a figure like a fruit on a plate,
black string around her neck
packaging a body of short French legs undressed
except for a high heeled slipper, an adornment
like the flower ribbon in her hair. Oh Olympia,
a courtesan, a whore, your picture, once moved
to hang high above the door, unseen
"like a spider on the ceiling."
Walk with this showing off of vulnerable flesh,
the yellow belly, the look beyond
the burning minutes of first "getting naked,"
time going by lying there,
not unlike those opalescent nudes
with pearl skin adrift on unreal waves,
light-dappled turn-ons who hide
the dark urges of a century's need
to believe that sex dances with death.
(They were so extravagant!)
An idea become more open on today's
selections on the internet,
its whispered Victorian sex like
the hidden fluttering of paper wings
while Olympia remains a calculated intellect —
self above love, self apart from love —
as, without passion, a digital black maid

holds out a flowery tribute to a woman
armored by her interest in woman,
though the viewer does not know that and,
thinks of her curious hazel eyes
as setting a price — no sentiments given,
no sentiments taken; paint is tougher than flesh —
as still the self comes in at eyes
that today will shine not with pruriency
but with the fresh curiosity
of a young girl's self-love.

MORISOT

Re: Berthe Morisot: 1841-1895

Picture this: She poses sharp featured,
carrying violets and cannot paint the nude,
cannot paint young girls on fainting couches
with one languishing dainty foot,
women like deer nested in the grass
dead nature laid out on a plate.
A sculptor shapes, like curved peacock tails,
round buttocks and fat breasts
while she stays at home, does women in pairs,
witnesses to each other, sisters in white dresses
and landscapes where trees are dressed,
seen from behind fences
by the demure hat, carrying violets
who holds a child's hand
and brooding, skirts swinging
must not paint the nude.

Looking down over the balcony,
holding the child's hand,
looking across the field,
holding the child's hand
looking, sitting in overdressed rooms
holding the child's hand
and from behind her easel
painting in the mirror.

Moving on to her next move,
drowning in those nets of sinking moods —
can she be as good as they?

She will paint the nude, hire faceless models
and, with fleeting strokes,
outline curving shoulders,
paint too full breasts
and now turns her back on supine female flesh.
Chin raised, demure, dark eyed,
she will paint and tear up,
paints in plein air,
paints child and friend and that self,
level eyed, in the fading mirror —
paints and paints.

EDEN

Something about La Grande Jatte
on Sunday afternoons when the world uncurls
and lines up under trees under which
half a lady fishes for pieces of color,
and a boat on the lake and its white sail
may be the whole story before everything shifts
to catch a wave among the upright backs,
under the bending trees, above dog, monkey,
girl in a white Sunday frock,
hat echoing the five open parasols
filling the air in a half step
of the movement of a watch.
Time like tinfoil on the green lawns of
La Grande Jatte. Remembering,
meanwhile, Central Park where
children in dungarees torn at the knees
and suited men sail their sons' small boats.
The divided touch becomes fractional
to stop the moment from sliding into the water
among the hum-humming of dots and motes
of light being juggled and nothing stopped,
of plus and minus equals under parasols where
what never happened keeps happening in sun and shade,
in gaslit sideshows or moments in the park.

THE SAD BEARDED JAPANESE EMPEROR OF MONTMARTRE

Though he builds up his arms with weights,
love is the main transaction
(not exchanges of the old franc or new dollar).
What woman can love a top-hatted dwarf
besides his mother? He has the answers:
With chalk, with zinc, with stone,
and inks that never wash off,
he twists the lips of Yvette Guilbert
and arranges meetings of half worlds,
where paper is a god-like receiver
of loving, spilled over breasts made
in the empire of Montmartre where
the dwarf manager orchestrates La Belle Epoque
in the dark and almost everyone makes money
amid the music of cash can do. Oh write me a letter!
Send the count's allowance,
to where costumed in public and private,
women in undress and very dressed,
sing under the dazzling fake daylight —
So fill up his glass, while dragging those legs
the music, the dancers. Fill up his glass,
he needs it by the barrel, time frame slipping,
shrinking — facts too tight a fit in photographs
as he changes faces, swells figures
yellow, olive green, purple and black —
all he has to give — Yvette Guilbert,
elongated gloved arms raking the curtain
sings where Jane Avril's snake thin body

stalks the moment, the stars of his galaxy
set free of reality even as the thick fingered
crippled woman tamer leaving a trail of paper
exits the scene.

CEZANNE AT HOME

How did he do it
painting against a dance of walls,
against the insides,
against those places of comfort
the inside of houses,
these objects that do not rest,
that make the mind shift to what is it
under the white cloth? Do you doubt him?
He doubts himself, the universe turning,
waiting on a white pitcher,
a bottle that does not fall, looking down
on tipped hidden tables,
drinking in the pitcher's lip,
the Bay of Estaque a bulging stomach,
the outside trees, a study
of nature vague on the details. He, he —
alone in the studio, with the brush
with the palette knife, with his life —
using three skulls to paint death,
painting light with a candlestick
to make of shifting glances,
unsteady seconds something as solid
as the throne of god
in which he once believed and doubts—
so tightfisted. Did the devil
have his ear? — knowing only nature and
wondering at every stroke
if it could be one more mistake —
or if stillness could be salvation brought to life,
in his motif, in the odyssey of days, of years
painting stone apples, onion tears,

an enduring interior so that
so you can live with a light blue vase,
a bent cloth on which sail
orange apples, pressing plates,
falling table covers
towering over weather and time —
illusions thickening to press
your lips on irregular cups.
Cezanne saying, every day is today,
painting away, painting away.

GAUGUIN REMEMBERING

I named the last hut, "House of Joy,"
painting the gold of their bodies,
the green tinged flesh —
painting the spirit of whose dead watching.
Painting wildness, walking
from those mysterious centers of thought
asking, Where do We come from —
myself, only my own voice —
Was I right? Positing this inner man posed
above and beyond a line of blue water.
Am I right? Purple, the perfume of the tropics,
behind the jar, the pipe, the fruit,
yellow flowers as lights in a room where
tacked to the wall are Hope and Olympia,
the old images like former brides,
Europe's aging wives, dreaming of Europe.
And will Paris applaud
the line of blue water, the denizens
of pink earth, brown gods,
and the less important, "easy" still lives —
my unstopping, shifting, shadowy still lives—
still life with sunflowers,
with Japanese print, with Hope,
that dull doll bleached white,
the ghosts of a life lined up —

Will they believe me
writing in endless letters of the gold of those bodies
of a mind and flesh dance in the tropical silence
of bulging flowers,
a self-portrait as severed head

become a clay pot filled with flowers
by the old man with a brush,
the paint still wet,
collecting seeds of the sun
and the short term of flowers, their sudden blush
the mind applauds and paints as permanent?
Dreaming, dreaming,
savage and Frenchman, liar and truth teller
naming my last hut "House of Joy"
in Tahiti or Paris never at home.

ANNUNCIATION AMONG THE IRISES

What's lost is the silence
needed to greet an angel for instance,
a silence that requires great formality
and spaciousness as he spreads his feathers
in a variety of colors,
touched with mordant gilt,
a kind of liquid gold,
a silica mixed in so that the wings
glitter with iridescent faith
as the angel Gabriel bows
beside column capitals and roof arches.
Architecture as order
as the saintly monk,
my heart, finds safety
in stone while Vincent —
Vincent prays, and wills himself to believe,
listening for dark tipped wings
to hover over his head,
comforting as music is comforting.
But today, poverty has lost its elegance,
its harmony, is remote like
a friar's vow of silence
in these rooms where red beard can't stop talking —
"The minor events of our lives tear us away
from meditations," he says and, losing himself,
paints blue irises pressed between black lines
of flower consciousness.

Unlike before, when Fra Angelico's fresco
echoed the annunciation that took place at dawn
when there was holy peace with the light

falling from the east where began each ordered day.
Now the light from the east is no longer measurable,
is full of uneven shadows,
is drunk up by clanging flowers.
And truth, the even tones, the belief
in the godly is hid safe
in a walled garden of peace,
in that painting of balancing of forces,
of woman and archangel intoning prayer,
the artist intoning painting as prayer,
a bowing in a garden ignorant of raw whites,
of the meaty blue and purples of plant flesh
and of Vincent houseless left — where is God? —
robbed of vanished halos and those mighty wings,
missing those figures still bowing
with hands crossed against the chest
to bring the light of day forward
while the irises, the irises
not quite reaching not touching
the sides of the canvas
are embedded in paths of sinuous black.
Moving across the paint's white meat
there are many, many annunciations:
"Poor Vincent. Such a genius," Pere Tanguy mourns.
"Poor Vincent. Are they masterpieces, yes or no?
And there are so many! And there are so many!"
as pictured here: where Mary and the angel are praying,
and the irises, the irises are screaming.

EXPRESSIONISM

He thinks of feelings like mountain peaks,
sees the body as a tree of
autumnal orange and the hope of yellow
in a landscape of rows of houses
with closed down windows.
Yesterday, Schiele traveled to hospitals
to learn the body's gestures;
brush moving, remembers every anguish
of sexual desire and proclaims the artist
a saint, needing not to be understood:
"The air I breathe will be famous,"
genius to genius, claiming Van Gogh's
sunflowers for himself. Before the mirror,
the body is a heap of sticks, he says,
arms lifting from the round earth;
apes himself and meditates upon
his greatness — young, young, young in a
preternaturally old November world.
At eighteen, nineteen, the women
bone and skin with breasts of barbed lines,
sex faced front unlike the painting
of himself as Crouching Man, his soul
become the angular body as he draws
his own aura. Will you understand?
The air is full, landscapes
full up to the top, the sun is gone;
we are all animals with whispered secrets,
hidden sins, victims of thin young girls
with old faces, the undersides of fat Vienna
he claims and draws himself pierced by arrows,
by the light that emanates from bodies

in the sweet air.
Poor boy, poor spoiled boy,
riding the wind, bony fingers evoking inner storms.
In sleep, crossing that dark river
to where the old king, your mad father
regularly entertains his imaginary guests.

LES DEMOISELLES D'AVIGNON

After Picasso

Posed for our waiting customers,
blue lights and pinkest skin
love is war as we group together
before the table, the fruit,
our secret slit —
Come, taste our perfumed sweat!
nudes with carved masks,
with five pairs of mismatched eyes
ugly and lovely equally sexy
looking to see you.
One nude sitting back to front
with monstrous mask,
an African medicine to cure your sickness
among bodies like rebuilt dreams,
a single hand, five fingers
flattened holding the wall
where love is war for witches
locked up in houses,
elegances of skin out of the sun —
oh, bleed for us,
who have the last laugh
on that street in Barcelona —

We demoiselles,
behind and in front of heavy curtains,
the painted images of Fernande and Laurencin
line up, arms behind —
taste our perfumed sweat,
as mothers of men's fantasies

against sky-blue stare out,
singing of Avignon, of a canvas circus,
of statuesque statues,
threatening as a room of welcoming women
who would and would not be tamed
lest the dog jump too high —
lest you fear all of us pretty ones
lurking in front of blue and red lights,
with those masks, those striving eyes,

Where from that bordello,
bordello is a more mellow word —
for that jungle of fear,
behind those walls,
unpacked from a box
the painted sum of his destructions
stand with distorted mouths,
posed for camera, for brush,
bodies turned inside out
to ask who threatens you.
— Dark animals standing as if lying down,
sharp angled giantesses, brazen faced
with staring eyes challenge;
we, a small man's love,
we five, the world's evil eye —
demoiselles of a murderous race —
other, other, and of that secret mirror,
the feminine, with pursed mouths
summon you.

IN THE BATH

After Pierre Bonnard

The bathroom is a fish bowl,
with tiles witnesses, like age under the mist,
in the blue and yellow air,
painted on glass, on canvas
where women's bodies
are lost boundaries, water logged under
yellow bands of sun,
sins are washed, fogged,
and omnipresent squares swim
above a tub's clawed feet
and nakedness dissolves, devolves
from whose shimmering scarf
dipped deep in a straggle of silk.
The body blue, the body yellow
floats in water
under the approach of sword-like brushes,
floats silently in a tub
while a small dog on the rug
hides in a square of light.

Screened by steam, blue shadows hover
over an open window filtering light:
"If we forget everything, only self
    is left," he said and
"it is still necessary to have a subject."
As twenty years after, he snaps her picture
and, in the tub's shadow,
claims Marthe must be abstract.

Where are the edges where so much light
becomes a kind of dark, a secret place,
hand in water becomes a theater
where, juice on the tip
of a thin brush dulls the scorings
of veins traveling to the outer reaches
of hands and feet through watery years
where you must not touch her, but hope
she can assume a privacy, a secret will
within the tile palace, the painter's
camera lucida.

Light follows the backside,
as a door always ajar jars the score,
blurs the face. Where and who
is the mirror, and who
the outside looker?
She must not think.
There is no escape even while
the standing yellow nude wears
outside shoes, resists the surrounding
yellow, stands still at the center —
until, on another canvas,
the air turns blue on aging flesh,
voiceless in fingers of air.
Light spins, weeks turn
and turn again and,
in yet another picture,
the artist returns her
to tub, coffin, shell,
to that prison boundary
of the boundaries of
her trapped and floating body.

MATISSE AND ICARUS

He finds his way —
returning through the breach,
he steps into pictures, knowing
a certain red affects the blood pressure,
knowing he cannot give up the body,
its systems of chair, hat, goldfish,
a window as picture found in conversation,
the bars of striped pajamas,
"not things but relations,"
arabesques of branches,
wall, floor, sliding together.
She in a blue chair, he in striped pajamas
fading into a wall of pictures
to see what happens to the plants
curls of green truth
distanced by red paint turning blue,
bodies of he and she turning blue —
sleep in blue far from trees
pictured in the window,
before doubling "with another density"
the red room, the red studio
recording daytime color —
shrinking of elements,
objects silenced, silenced all his struggles.
Are they, were they the only reality
for bathrobe conversation?

"We are fed up with so much skill."
Painting, he no longer talks of skin,
but of unearthly seamless pink
timbres of concentration,

awkwardnesses, body flattened
framed in blue tile.
"Everything that is not useful.
Fit your parts into one another —
the body, the body!
meaning shadow on the wall,
figure on the canvas stretching,
using black to cool the blue
and after years and years of
odalisques like a beautiful chair,
see him drowning in her body
and, needing rescue,
escape to Tahiti where only
Gauguin's wounded vanity kept him awake.

Matisse, too, works out of solitude and boredom.
Fifteen years later, remembering the ocean,
the ocean as a blue word rising
in the silver light of Nice,
as sea horse and starfish,
scissors cutting out swimmers
in remembering Tahiti
retaining only what?
Matisse, Matisse cutting into color
the color of ideas. His Icarus,
a black shape rising, blue cooling black.
What cannot be seen carried by the light,
black Icarus rising, floats up
through blue air.

CUT WITH A KITCHEN KNIFE

After Hannah Hoch

She wakes up every morning a new woman.
Yesterday, with a sharp scissors she cut out female legs.
 Today, there are sales everywhere,
pictures in newspapers mounting up.
What did she know building her
ethnographic museum of mutilated girls
"cut with a kitchen knife?"
Her face fades surrounded by pictures of men marching.
Hear the sounds of their feet. The Nazis are coming.
In photographs, her face fades into her lover's
who tells her marriage is the amplification
of rape. Then, afterwards, she meets a woman.
Much later, soldiers come and leave her
digging up her garden of Dada plants,
burying deep her archives of art.
And always she goes on, unconsumed by love,
pasting together fractured features, pieces of self.
Was she proving that nothing matches?
Paste and mend: See, how a man's face
held aloft by pigeon's wings flies down the street,
how a saw rests across a sleeping woman,
a ballerina, her head turning
balancing on top of a doll's twirling feet,
a dance of hands while four men's masks worry
the blue twilight of a sky growing from the ground,
the bottom of someone's shoes rises, soaring —
in an underground breathing Dada air
gathering and pasting together
man, woman, roof, and cat's paw.

SYNTHETIC CUBISM

Magic, new magic — "Would he like it,
would, would he?" fat Gertrude asks.
"The sense of not making sense, be with you."
Apollinaire sings from an airplane.
Would she, would she like it,
taking things apart, feeling all sides
with your eyes? If I told him, if I told her,
the way the boys did it, the way she wrote,
all the clocks in the world crawling toward
the same hour when they did it, made it
like mountain climbers lashed together
scaling the heights of painted trees
and guitars. Up, up, up the incline
of a century with train tickets and Le Journal
the sky turning red, filling up
so it's hard to breathe?
Well, what isn't time travel? Gertrude mocks,
if not Braque and Picasso
sitting down to breakfast materials
a pipe, a glass, a knife,
the news of every day black and white dramas,
refracted light, tan with broken
triangles and diagonals, violins of space,
flying shadows, edges of feeling
lashed together. Did they like it, like
the Spanish guitar, like the French violin,
signaling nature can be rearranged
learned through our finger ends
sounding in space as the twentieth century begins
measuring four-sided moments
feeling with four-sided fingers,

"one is certainly doing something,"
stopping and starting.
Long live Cubisme
still new and no wiser
as the twentieth century ends.

FUTURIST COOK-UP

Smell the poem, eat the picture —
said four young men in flapping coats,
who had between ages 30 and 40
before outlawing spaghetti
and dining on paintings in carpeted galleries —
a good time being had.
I am not a futurist but know how
an argument too is a good time
when there is no one left to hit.
Help yourself to it under the beautiful blue.
In an ocean of voices run together,
my heart aches after elegant boots
but nothing makes anything better.
The men hold up plate glass emotions because
among the water of voices calming,
under the beautiful blue, being Italian in excess,
they are allowed to cry in public,
World War II creeping up.
Here is the lesson of the interregnum:
Wait on the next wave,
and while counting losses, heat up the sauce.

MONDRIAN

Mondrian, the utopian swan,
a life of square forms
of patterns of silent color gliding.
equal equals equal. — Shall we dance,
in a country of windmills,
above and beyond likenesses,
loving only the pure idea
of windows and blushing church tower,
all frames through which you see
the spatial, three dimensional presence?
Harmony, the sounds of wings, a bend of wind,
the red moment — what we have in common
submerged in the universal
electric of red yellow and white
that blazes up in *Victory Boogie Woogie*.

Go back.
After leaving Paris, he builds
on emptiness, staring at landless sea,
watching stepping water levels,
the sound — what you can't make up;
pluses and minuses like ink scratches
in paintings of sums like suns.
Equal equals equal
from diamond shaped windows,
dark to light as in country to country,
in France, in England
the sky changes, light to dark, as with
thickening and thinning bands,
with nailed down marks
he changes his measures.

A shadow glides above the water.
Is this the future, windows into doors
a right angle grid become a right
angled god? I will sing rule
is order, measure. Shall we dance —
box steps, side steps,
fingers detailing heart beats
in equilibriums of music —
red and yellow sounds equaling movement,
equals equaling movement
gliding, gliding under the bird's wing.

DE CHIRICO'S AFTERNOON METAPHYSICS

A clean sweep in a square bordered by empty avenues,
eyes in my hands, at the wide corner of 57th Street,
the tall young man, dealing in presentiments,
announces, "We're all living in the tomb of Khufu."
"Yes," I say, acknowledging this final meeting,
"yes, but I have to catch the Fifth Avenue bus."
And riding home, the talk evaporating
I remember the forgotten silence
pressed against the sides of buildings,
and see De Chirico where the rubber glove
hangs nailed to the wall as trains come
and go in the waiting tomb of Khufu
where nothing will happen except maybe on the wall
a shadow interfering with the young girl with a hoop
who runs up, up the incline of early morning.
Hope transforms into architecture,
a sliding down of the great pencil,
the green baseball, the white arches and
nailed down boxes whose secret thoughts
escaped to unbalance him,
the sides of buildings appearing
among translations of pages of philosophy,
scenic dream sequences, setups of pale wine.
Sip, sip the bitter red from raffia-wrapped bottles
as clear-skinned and waving cigarettes,
we bite the clock. The black haired man disappears,
growing older, the shapes of windows down the street
change, young memories skipping away
like puffs of smoke, like De Chirico at twenty-two,

singing of wrong-way trains
with nothing behind or before
and no direction to build upon
but the melancholy of invented departures.

ADIEU TO YOU TOO, MARCEL

The urinal is here, so
where are the sinks of yesteryear?
Chair moves. A wheel humming,
the ineffable chocolate grinder
listening nun-like on the shelf.
Time stays and virgins go flying
in pursuit of swift nudes,
a retinal smell, one-night stays
and day-leavings, glass breakings
and dust breeding.
Oh Rrose Selavy, your glory
is to be two in one,
knowing that love is, will be and has been the fourth dimension.
"The fact he is standing up in a more or less vertical way,"
nine bachelors, nine malic modes hanging in air is art, isn't it?
Tasty as chocolate? Meanwhile or because
the illuminating gases of blind desire
spill from the notes, with a touch of malice
doubly knowing, of the green box
to move the pistons of imagination.
My chance, my chance,
he will say and sign for everything.
"Dada is as useless as everything else."
And oh Rrose Selavy, love is, will be,
and meanwhile has gone dancing in the fourth dimension.
What is it you are keeping between your hands?

WITH HIS EYES CLOSED

"I paint what cannot be photographed.
I photograph what I do not wish to paint."
Man Ray

An iron tears at my clothes.
The lips of the sofa press together.
Do you love me, love me?
The hopes of a very young man and
maybe she is not a coat stand,
spin the camera.
Shadow of shadows of the rope dancer
in red, yellow, and green —
his dream of another future.
Reverse, reverse:
"I photograph what I do not wish to paint,"
he said, shutters shut and opening
on white velvet hours.
In the dark room, he said,
where is the "I" in your eye?
Is it lost in objects weighed down
by their own shadows,
by white pearls, by the rayograph
of an arm before she disappears
into a tower of silver beads?
Her eye is the spear of a metronome
on the last stop of the metro.

An armada of coat hangers advances.
"I photograph what I do not want to paint,"
he says. Are paintings more real than photographs —
twenty years in Paris with a Brooklyn accent.

It's all just a picture. And thinking,
what of thinking? Brickbats of words,
denuded images reclothed.
Is it time to celebrate that
which is wrapped and roped
in a blanket as mystery while
art runs ahead past the sewing machine
  and umbrella
escaping into the lips of a sofa
where Alice, Gertrude, and Marcel press together?

LES JEUX SONT FAITES*

For Renée Magritte

Art is my game, painting stories with wrong endings:
a room of tiny chairs and tables where
a giant rose explodes and it wasn't a dream
the day my mother in her nightgown
jumped off a bridge — Oh, Ophelia floating
down the river! — while I paint a fish
standing on women's legs and memory as blood
gushing from a marble head, the logic
of loss running free offers a kind of liberty
in the garden of my delights where
what is not becomes a question of truth
sliding from under a bowler hat.

And I dream day turns off night's electric lights
to light the darkness of a mind, a pocketbook
of thought which, if not the world, is what,
I say, as under wrapped faces the eye learns to feel
and violent loss sees through blind cloth
to straddle that bird of pampa grass
(save me, save me!)
offering a kind of liberty to a lonely boy
hedging his bets when les jeux sont faites —

and I am what is left, wrapped in too tight memories,
publishing thin smiles in furnished rooms
in which the furniture fights back
and everything is flat, flat, flat —
and still the wrong way is the better way
as the die are dancing and you join up.

My grief gone dancing as les jeux sont faites
and I paint what I think while
an army of men in bowler hats
fill up a sky bereft of cottony white pumped up clouds,
of beautiful blue and white pumped up clouds.

*The croupier's phrase meaning 'the dice are thrown' or 'the game has been played.'

MAGIC SHOW

For Luis Bunuel

At eighty, he wrote of the whispering
of the middle ages of his childhood
to hold off death with a five-year-old's fantasies
of pursuing spiders with bloody fingers,
and those faces behind walls, before anyone,
especially him, made a box to hold them.
Wholeness is an opening for damage as,
between the tinkle of glasses,
those broken tears on the bathroom floor
he likens to the sound of church bells,
people marching through giant corridors,
a failed ending for the long movie,
his magic show where well dressed people
at a never-ending party iron their clothes
unable through days and weeks
of flickering light to leave — even as
in dim bars, blonde hair is shining silver.
Dear Luis, as a priest now waits
to close your eyes in Christ,
you don't pray but write of
your sister, of how high below
your shoulder she stood in secret games
resting, fluttering like a bird,
that small hand almost touching my cheek
as the postman on his bike pulls up
beside the bed with a satchel
of messages from you
who stopped here. Was it long enough?
Old man, old man, the bells are ringing
reel after reel, the camera always on.

GEORGIA ON MY MIND

Collecting shadows where a grinder grinds
in the broken silence behind
a tree shape between sky and ground.
Going from Sun Prairie, Wisconsin, across
the Texas plains. I read someone defined
American as one who moves around as easily
as crowds ride in subway cars touching while
holding on to unseen, open, untouchable space
so she saw and loved shape,
and impassible distances encompassing the eye.

With no one to ask what do they think of me,
Georgia, small lady, wanders
knowing loneness as precious distance
seeing arms of two red hills reaching,
seeing giant flowers like foreign faces,
city buildings wearing necklaces of windows,
where the people are invisible
and the dream is to walk through winter snow
    like desert sand.

Black and white (what she wore)
painting an unending brown curve
    downhill to disappear,
painting color as "significant language,
abstract as fact." At the start,
under the camera staring, asking
what does he think of me posed
in dated white and black.

I wonder who that person is, she said
to his record of restless hands, fingers
at play, unbound hair, head turned away.
"She, she's a purer form of myself,
Steiglitz said, seen under a hat,
examined part by part.
Important to find the artist in the art,
the woe in the woman looking away.

A grinder grinds in the broken silence.
What is the color of summer heat grown older,
the colorings of dust clouding an empty sky
of baking and drying sun? Until finally,
she went where painting crosses is
painting the country, a hot state of equivalences.
and she all in white under red and orange hills.
goes back past black and white,
circles back to what she saw drowning in color,
cartwheeling red canna,
flailing peony, shameless hollyhock,
shy lily petals opening—
"I am I,"—they say, "Look at me,"
her long bones walking up the hill.

FRIDA'S FEET

Everything is extreme: love, pain
and there are days I cannot walk,
but there is always the mirror,
the water, and living the coupling
of delicate dove and fat frog, and all
those years of Frida, in the bathtub,
toes like thumbs, like secret vices
love can't always help. In the bathtub,
leaning back to see images of those feet,
of a pierced shell, a dead bird
of the parents of my history like tears
floating underwater. In the bathtub,
those red toes and WHAT THE WATER GAVE ME —
dreams all memories hidden under long skirts,
one leg shorter and thinner than the other,
two eyebrows become one and
nothing made up as I paint myself
in half portraits under Diego's green eyes,
hands dealing in love, feet in pain
hobbling across every heart
while painting a wounded heart
alongside an empty dress,
painting Frida with the long hair,
Frida with Diego's face as third eye,
Frida holding up a broken spinal column
and painting the bloodied figure of one
whose lover gave her A FEW SMALL NIPS.
I am not alone, mi amor
during stumbling reunions with Diego,

my faithless lover and loving son,
— *mi corazon, mi corazon. Here*
I am together with images of myself
laid at the bare feet —
so far from heaven, so close to America —
of Mexico and Rivera.

POLLOCK AMONG THE NAVAJOS

"On the floor I am more at ease. I feel nearer, more
part of the painting since this way I can walk around
it, work from the four sides. . .This is akin to the
Indian sand paintings of the West."
Jackson Pollock,
"My Painting, *Possibilities, 1947-48*

Slash and burn, drinking up
the empty roads of Wyoming,
moving with oil, enamel, aluminum paint
shaken from sticks, forced
through holes of tubes, cans,
into moving lights, line rhythms,
to where pictures are magic writing for curing,
or they help, they help.

And watch the trickling
of dried vegetable colors
into rows of figures, armies
of snakes, clusters of stars,
pick-up sticks.
Making requires order,
long lines of arrows, of eagles
into straight lines of feathered figures —
medicine man with prayer sticks,
Jackson bleeding with brushes, cans, paint sticks —
hearing footsteps across sand paintings
where they sprinkle meal and
cover what remains around the smoke hole.

They want to photograph him painting,

film the hidden narrative.
Body sweating, rocking
as they take his picture —
so we can see you, steal that face —
that knows movies are a wrong-way mirror,
that in drinking there is no salvation,
and still fills up with chaos and alcohol,
needing to find a lost medicine,
needing to find a magic that will cure him.

Birds patterning the sky,
the ground, and row on row
are boundaries. Measure them while
snakes assist in the ascension
with cures for bear sickness,
for mental disturbance, for the poison
of snakes and arrows.

And see painting restore order,
a ceremony of curving lines, arcs of black,
balancing of winds of aluminum paint,
structures of white veins,
thickets of planned gestures,
like and unlike those paintings of armies
of snakes and eagles, of stillness
in an unmoving sky, even as he stoops
to earth to dip and pour, trace on the floor
footprints to no more weeping,
to the sharpness of the moment moving.
Order, order, figures below the surface marching,
hands to the sky — no up, no down direction
like Indians singing.

THEY WILL TAKE MY ISLAND

For Arshile Gorki

Needing to dream of Lake Van,
needing to be someone else,
seeing with mournful eyes that were never young,
scrubbing the floor and going on long walks
with the ghosts of other artists
"I, Arshile, mellifluous in my choice
of names whose dreams form the bristles of
my artist's brush," collect shapes,
a dainty foot like a cartoon imp,
a green stride, shapes of apricots and dates
blazoning red on red soldier audiences,
my Armenian mouth delivering lies,
claiming every landscape Khorkom,
that California equals Armenia. Why not?
A love of line wandering off
between thought and talk.
I do not know me, artist painting
a brightening crowded garden,
painting the memory of embroidered aprons
and head scarf, rock salts of pain,
and charred beloveds of blushing color.
They will take my island,
immigrant painter chanting
flesh is lost and sadness continues,
singing abysses of an inner search,
singing where the cow jumps,
singing findings from the heavy lidded
eyelids of another land.
Bereft, left to celebrate in paint

crowned figures, animal masks,
marching reds, forms within forms,
my fears on which I have lived too long:
mother and son in an old photograph
fading into the whiteness of new painting,
little lost boy standing under the light,
they will take my island —
shape in the water, heart in the mouth,
flesh in my sight, take what I have sung,
what I have painted — my tendernesses gather up.

THE DUTCHMAN'S UGLY WOMEN

After Wilhem De Kooning

Feet spreading out of high heeled shoes.
Woman, a natural disaster erupts
across the canvas on which he paints
images in messy paint strokes
like a bar's cigarette smoke, black goddesses,
are pictures not of what he remembers but who
he knows under the past's faces,
the equivalent of earlier brown dreams
of love and alcohol and her in the bar,
rosy and fat, on oak thighs not to be
pulled apart. So drink, drink, drink
to monster mothers, to monster nightmare females
and crucifixion figures.

Why did he think monster females funny,
a crazy cartoon story? Was it funny
that a fifty-year-old man agonize
over his home-breaking mother,
eyebrows shooting out over black bulb eyes
as she broke his bows and arrows when he was five
leaving his funny bone twitching —
until now it no longer hurts to laugh —
which he does in his paintings.

Yes it's always about power
on new roads and old
as huge, breast-plated women
with rows of gnashing teeth,
his warriors of the night kick out.

Not what he saw, crossing the ocean
but what he found in brighter air:
"America I love you. Goddesses
with pairs of blood red mouths,
your young girls with wide throated "T-zones,"
"tight" skirts, your Carols,
Marilyns or Elaines — something to hold onto
inhaling middle-aged evenings of alcohol,
while taking apart the body: the, her,
building "shes" of stabbing strokes,
flesh cushions and pillow stomachs,
representing the absence
of something to lie down on,
as he makes sex, sex, sex
be outraged by time's mirror in which
he dissolves the warm pink, the blue, the yellow,
melding his colors — touch earth — because
this loved and hated flesh is always landscape.

MARK ROTHKO IN THE INNER STUDIO

For Markus Rothkowitz 1903-1970

Subject matter: The Timeless and the Tragic.
Except inside and outside the studio,
who can you trust—only Markus
seeing meanings in reds and yellows,
seeing the pleasure of anguish in a paint stroke,
and pondering how God hid his light behind
a burning bush. The painting, a praying
with blocks of color.
The message conveyed by gentle blurs,
that you wake to see as each day's light
eats away the morning's edges until
you catch shadow castles reflected
in the darkened window
of a building with stairs
that maybe Kafka climbed.
Seeing as a way of scaling mountains,
arriving in America at age ten
over a swirl of sea to meet
thieves here too who steal
from Jews, and in the pit
of self-loathing, you
set traps for the sun.
Learning in the dark shades,
the exultations of browns and blacks
and what is singular about purple,
what is winter about red.
Oh blushes, moments of change,
rushes of blood, the burning bush.
Repeat, repeat after me that threnody of childhood

of the presence of God,
of the ocean, of the East River calling.
Go, put the money in a drawer,
a having without seeing.
Don't count, take yourself by surprise.
You are not Nathan the Wise as
your *"a little drinkin' helps the thinkin',"*
eliminating abstract figures
from a wave of washes,
Markus become Mark
the sun at half-mast,
the shades descending,
your internal temperature blazing,
the paintings now dark sharers —
invented shadows of He-who-might-be
pushed on, pushed farther
to reach the light over the water.

EVIL OMEN

Poetry as chessboard, as marked off shore
looking for its own history,
he thinking about that Greek who sailed away
in these pictographs that are
the evil imagination of his good eye.
Here his visual spells above the clock on the bed
underlines, overlines and nowhere to hide
in what would be an incantation,
of sunbursts and frozen sounds
in cubicles mapping the presences
of terror and fear.
The painter paints the eye of Oedipus
before the door closes
on fainting blues,
a paratactic meaning,
pockets of stones,
air, water, fire in deeper blue-greens,
his drawing with closed eyes
sailing, sailing, sailing on
to smaller ports of entry
inside yourself
where the windows are shut
and there is nothing to read
or hold in your hand
beside this bad luck charm,
this bug made of shifting color,
an icon in a dark field of things worn and weathered
in night voyages from desert browns and yellows
until eyes shift and see,

walls of smiling hand-prints — watch your back —
internal steps, the evil imagination of his good eye
following, following.

IN SEARCH OF THE REAL

After Hans Hofmann

Hans gathers up all the fictions
of the studio, a deaf German,
who paints naked, making his
purple-lined red squares
into balancing blocks of light
and knowing sunsets haven't to do with art,
believing color is hope,
while lovely nudes line up
to be pinned down and
flatten my paper heart.

Hans, Hans plays the perpetual teacher,
"Paint makes for illusions, paint is real"...
my large flat planes serve as pillars."
Oh immensity, immensity!
like the crescendos of California.
And where is home, he asks in
that heavy accent.
Bring me to blue water
where my eye travels the earth's curve
leading students on parallel paths,
telling them stories of great men
on parallel paths.
Energy, energy! See how
the sky is a mighty theater
in the search for abstract order.

And each time, yellow skies and green
walk the tops of trees

and hands reach for the real
as forms are put down and wiped away —
until finally in Provincetown she dies
and he is left alone with the empty waves,
and then, what of color intervals
while the sun inches along,
and what of plasticity, spirituality
and the new reality, he taught?
Begin. The canvas is an opening
to taste, touch, feel space
as lost in the perception of hidden laws,
he marries again at eighty-five
and goes on painting.

THE BEATIFIC BANANA PEEL

Caught between museum walls,
swimming in air, the Calders soar
and hover, sun and moon
beyond where balance matters.
Finger by finger, things in air
share a further space
where a fin of strips shiver
and the work of the fat red-faced magician,
the work of an admirer of wasp-waisted,
blade-thin beauty, the mind's acrobat
sets his weights afloat creating
unhinged train cars that slip their locks
and pop goes the finny tail. Purse your lips,
and it's back to the house and the run
of schedules across which a breath
sends a blade moving into worlds on wires.
Purse your lips. The body knows
there's no such thing as falling upward
into the unsteady stars. I turn and turn,
and in soaring pratfalls, beautiful arcs
become my body, and in these metal shapes,
a slip beyond a skid or the uncalculated jump
of the comedian cat can bring a free fall
into fractal space where red and black
shadows intersect on an earth doing
an unseen dance. Bring on the drinks,
Alexander. Today I will look away
from where (all this is off the street)
they spin so slowly, so slowly
as falling caught up in fear
I lose the dream of soaring

and my bones turn to water
as falling means losing the earth
and biting the crust
on which I daily stand.

NEVELSON

Down long corridors, living
so long she manages to be old,
knowing everything about shapes,
making halos of the Madonna from toilet seats
darling, darling, love always secondary...

Darling, darling, move the crate to the left.
Simplifying, simplifying.
In time, one forgets the unnecessary
and everybody's name becomes "darling.
And about forms: She programs
you to walk into a moon garden.
Accept will you — love always secondary —
can you see anything of which
you are not already aware?
Looking from under fur eyelashes,
she gives anger's answers
to the impertinences of living.
Implacable circles, dawns, and dusks
are not only objects,
but the in-between places,
structures drawing
as they drive her.

Behold imaginary willow cabins
to see inside:
the glory of seeing built
from an altar of thought.
This willow cabin,
the air we breathe,
the color of darknesses,

a wedding of balustrades,
facing out breaking your sight;
her architecture of shadows
rejecting God in favor of holy shapes,
not wood but feeling
from parts of old furniture.

And raging, raging,
assembling her soldier columns,
her horizontal pilings,
constructivist looking glass shapes,
tall as a queen,
remembering all the silences of being ignored,
tall as a queen,
oh majesty, oh rule of wood
long shadows in the autumn air,
trees the interstices of light,
blocks and cylinders,
clusters of cubes, black fronts
still with the appearance of a universe.

That hammer in hand, grasp is meaning,
self an army of shapes,
walls and wedding chapels,
the symmetry of black moons and
sky cathedrals.
darling, darling, move it there.
Oh ugly trees and sober walls,
She marries wood,
she manages eighty years of
unbalanced ambition.
What she, what I can do while you
buy my work, be my hands,

making pieces places
tall as a queen,
darling, darling
these ugly trees, these pieces places
face us down.

PAINTING AT NIGHT

In an empty heart, "If beauty is only
sometimes truth and sometimes not,
why paint?" the gavel-voiced judge asks,
for whom lying is a life and death matter,
whose invisible robes lie heavy, heavy,
and who judges even as I, his daughter,
pour my paints in diaphanous veils,
from colors of deceit create aureoles of truth.

Last night the blond moon was divided perfectly.
And though he is gone — who walked so lightly,
so lightly — I am still his daughter.
"Law is the most perfect science: Blind,"
he says and I continue to pour as the landscape pales
lacking my green suns (Paints are rough, ropy skeins
to be controlled), as tonight, in a terrifying wind,
I pick my way through uptown streets and walk across
orderly cement which will remain inviolate.

Lonely now — through all those shut doors,
be polite, he says, a long shadow on the street,
calling liar, liar in the wind — even as lovers follow after,
the cold is warm, a storm in this pigment
become a lasting stain while streets do not change
and trees leaf the same. Understand, inviolate space
is what in thirty years I find soaking, drawing.
(Is this deceit?) It's how things get done
on canvases more delicate than skin.

Close the door. Leave the father/daughter
masquerade, skate across this yellow,

ride the poured blue and do not talk of truth,
judging, judging. You had your word skill, logic,
so never mind what I traded for what
mountains and rivers. Like you, I give myself
the power — these canvases sing. Eyes fixed on me,
judge not, father, I have freed myself
and made a space to rest the mind.
Don't leave me, don't leave me
while using this paint and paper
to get me through my life.

THE REIGN OF ART AND ARDOR

Reign, reign, little queen far from France.
La la, Louise! La la!
Witness of sex through table legs,
awake and asleep feeling its thunder.
Woman explorer, who runs her hands
across marble, rubber, shaping pendulous breasts,
vagina houses walking on legs,
who believes in men and in self-betrayal,
sticks sticking from her heart,
groups together her portable brother —
Carry on, carry with you those people
you knew and missed,
in the studio building plank by plank.
"Men are our mirror"
and Ain't I a woman? Not bourgeois,
but Bourgeois! Born of his rib,
small and brittle, bearing and now bereft
of three enormous children,
emerging from a house
whose hidden openings lie down again and dream.
Sons gone, the fist of parental love closes in on itself
and childhood is now the only minute
before feasting on oneself. In all these places,
what is landscape? Bodies at the second half
looking back to when they were small and
witnessing the destructions of the father.
Double sexed icons, recrudesences
strewn apart like headless rabbits
recalling your or someone's birth and
the blind feeding of the young growing
and growing in place. Royalty, loyalty.

Even as you build, family is a crowd scene:
See how they surround as you shape in ugly turnings
those boxed assortments of breasts,
love's rolling hills and openings to keep before your eyes.

ART PROCESS

For Eva Hesse, 1936-1970

Ring around your rosie, little Eva,
sculpting those funny red breasts,
going to extremes, using plastic webs like dried cat guts
as something to swing on, fueled by a ladder of anger,
beautiful stranger, immigrant intensity,
boiling all down to a feeling for ropes
and teguments, scatterings on floor, industrial remnants,
to frames of pain, pushing further
a need to laugh, asking what else is art made of,
making those absurd frames of pain that
took you beyond that flowering tumor,
a translucent curtain, shutting down your future.

See on the wall
Hesse's cannibalizing of her own history
 the tensile anxiety of nerve and bone
in strings and circles to make a hole she went through
to find a lost self in meetings of tongue and groove;
art and love going round, giving a circular spin
to the gatherings of grievings,
the joinings of fanatic pain flowering
on these walls she left — in which maybe
she did live long enough to use up her life.

AGNES THINKING ABOUT GOD

After Agnes Martin

Nothing moves but the sand, and the line
of desert floor. Holy, holy, holy,
woman into mountain, an unmoving cloud,
my hair clipped short, solitary,
believing art a line,
a road for absolute clearance.

Look at that long reach
of plain in this flat country
where "mesa" means tableland;
ocher and tan bleach pink, and white light on
sand is a delicate drawing,
these rolling grains, mathematics made
into a kind of music of stop and go.

See my bisecting lines. These are the only crosses
a Christian girl can have who goes
beyond religion and, believing in shedding a skin,
cuts through the terrible weight
of familial ties to seek another
kind of love, a desert that thinks in centuries.

And moving beyond loneliness
discovers shifting rhythms of white
while the roadrunner, head down, oh prescient bird,
sees beyond its body. Is this how to become a saint,
Agnes, making your mark a litany in the noon light
where lizards and prairie dogs discover god in themselves?

STELLA, THE STAR

Up close, silvery aluminum. Sequins glitter, colors splash.
Up close, why is ornament heartless, like the architectural curve
that can and will bend all ways? The beginning, lines and straight
diagonals, green piano keys to be found summoning loss.
Loss of Russian constructivists in beginnings made for lost Polish
synagogues in faded photographs. Here, complex wooden buildings
made for prayer. And now, what we see is more, what we get is less
as Frank Stella the Star trusts only what escapes his hand, aiming
to rebuild the color flash of bird and motor car.

What's enough? A French curve in a play of Mary or Marilyn
and sexier slithering down a painting runway? At MoMA, the world of
goddesses go round. You want a tap dance to mean more than sound and
light and grace? Down below ground Stella dances. Above, Matisse's
goldfish swim and mean. Distance art to touch the eye, which is the mind,
fingers restless, so see Stella better from the hall, while Ana Mendietta
has other evidence. Ana's artist fingers draw paths of blood.
The Caribbean, the African, the borrowed underworld throbs through
Matisse and Picasso and the etched magnesium of Stella graffiti. She, the night
side, the "passed away" deaths and murders of more than slaughtered trees.

Stella's Brazilian birds and Mendieta's *siluettas*, visual sound
that takes the measure of breath. Twentieth century splendor —
the hand-print on mud or magnesium, the artist's only message
whatever writers say. Prayer animals in caves, Stonehenge astronomy,
and now the art exchange. $57 Million for Van Gogh's madness lied about
in faded reproduction. What was it he saw even as the paint cracks?
No matter. Somewhere a light goes on, and the dream record continues.

WHAT SHE CAN EXHIBIT: A Dance for Lynda B:

Being Greek, she remembers the body's meaning
when marble goddesses wore technicolor skins
and spins from herself colored lakes,
fingers of nightmare, a polyurethane meltdown
of marblized veins calling out, dance, dance!
And discovers sex today is a sea of cells
humming in her ears, discovers how salty blood tastes,
affirming we are here and enjoying someone else's pain —
curtsy to the right. Her arm reaching,
gesturing at what is internal, external
and vulnerable — my yellow nails, your purple tongue —
while she struts and paints remember me,
remember me and turn, turn!

Never trust an artist: She is a liar,
a cheat, a betrayer who leaves up
on the wall intricate knots that
open doors for the mind,
twistings shaping the moment's widening space,
parading the moment's widening space as
what we can have: Glory, glory! show us the way!
Tropical rain forests come apart
and decoration equals defiance
as she goes beyond bravery to
allure, a non-logical activity,
green eye shadow, gold nose ring,
sequin temples, a new religion
filling her hands where false jewels shine real.
And in my heart, we are grateful
for this price fixing, this break in the circle
that may be all that art can give:
Dance, dance and turn and bow!

FROM THE OTHER SIDE OF THE MIRROR; HER PICTURES

After Cindy Sherman

Collected here, the pathos of the blonde in the rain,
the dark one lying on the bed under the light,
breasts half exposed, hiding a hurt.
It's a job, and maybe because the more
they like her, the uglier I make her,
lying head down, alien, staring
from these pictures in frames, in magazines
where I hide, head disguised
in blond, brown, red wigs, uncombed,
supplying shards of glass, bits of what is
in smooth, smooth photographs
shattering someone else's high glossed fantasies.
Are pictures a putdown? No, no:
We spend years learning to be doll faced —
In dress up for girls, the three-year-old turns
seven in a pink tutu, diaphanous, see-through,
ignorant of the beating feet, the sweat you catch
that are really tears on the ballerina's face.
Have you caught on too, how girls are never old,
that the reproach of faces starts later,
as here where I am my own stand-in
aping an arrangement of eyebrows,
the anger of mouths, turning the head
of the girl with her suitcase by the road
or standing in the hall outside a furnished room,
listening to the jingle of coins
blank and familiar in the dark,
head half turned, lighted under colored gels

paper thin, poised on walls, in made-up camera skin
standing false, unknown and free
in the street, in the kitchen, isn't this being woman?
I am not I, but what I make you see.

WORSHIP

Clarity is overrated for me,
having come from a wild country,
where today once again, I return in my mind
to claim my territory,
to make art as a record,
as a memory, as solid weight
to keep the soul from straying.
In the woods I was alone
with the sound of brushing waters,
the sleeves of fog around my shoes
seeking the gestures of childhood
as something maybe to keep and honor.
Twenty years later, I build a box
of cement and wood
and arrange the hidden insides
to keep invisible time.
A box (or body) is a stop
in someone's path,
like on that old mud walk
where I held to myself, almost balanced,
spine like a rope straight up.
Look at this box sitting on the floor,
held by bandaged sticks,
in its own space deaf
to trains, subways,
biting copper wire singing,
deaf to the outside.
I wrap time inside square fences,
preserving hours in boxes,
living between latticed levels
pressed together as today

the wind rises.
Look now, I have boxed in the sky,
made repetition into strips of prayer,
restored my wild country.

THE WOMAN IN THE GROUND
(for the sculptor Ana Mendieta who fell from
a high window in 1985)

        How far do you go back, how far did Ana go back?
Everything begins in landscape, bark prints,
her imprint, the silueta, her sculptures in the land,
that drawing, a core of moving black branches,
insect legs or arms so small from Ana —
a falling doll, a Cuban doll
like one brought from Guatemala,
blue skirt, shining beads, tan skin,
become a dream of dolls.
Listen to the Havana Spanish
from the spider's mouth as her tree
and root call for a father too late,
torn from her country, traveling to
Iowa, Florida, Rome to peer in dark mirrors
that drink up her face and dance —
bone roots, blood from trees.
She, she, ai, ai! Spread on floor,
the imprint of arms, each word a grave
for that body that measured in hand spans
less than five feet and lay claim,
understand, to Cuba, her Atlantis.
She mirrored in her altars of sand,
sprinkling gun powder and the hope of fire,
crying, how do you live apart from
where you are born? My land —
mesas and mountains of a woman's body,
stories, stories, ma vida
Ana, my Ana, your losses cooled in alcohol.
She, she, ai, ai! Chair cracks, clay cracks,

memory offers and we take back
bits and pieces: the fall,
the blood path of her sculptor lover,
a man like a mountain looking down
at Ana, the thrown away doll.
She, she, ai, ai, death takes all but the land.

VENUS-INTRA-VENUS

For Hannah Wilke

"To be beautiful is not to come unstuck.
Beauty dies. We All die," said Hannah,
naming herself, Venus-intra-Venus, her own movie star,
who took on all the muses in thousands
of pictures made talking non-stop,
white skinned and with a killing Brooklyn accent;
her imagery, the pure silence of her features
heard in photographs of that body clothed in nakedness.
Always the sex thing: Leg raised, aiming her toy gun
in endless tapes — over and over —
a 4-year-old's coyness, waving her body like a flower,
whose "images of me with my mother"
recorded what cancer did to that other generation.
Steel skinned, she mailed out her chewing gum vaginas,
a feared female marauder asserting,
that if sex was good, sex with beauty must be better,
talking nonstop in that killing accent
that wouldn't let you get away.
Here recorded posing, standing on the bed,
a hospital sheet about her hips, holding with
still beautiful round arms the vase of flowers on her head,
a bloated bandaged Hannah, hair drawings on walls,
paper vaginas on the floor mourning what she will not have.
Wilke unwilted, Venus-Intra-Venus still the star
flashes her ass, uncovering her cancer for the camera.

FAITH

In fogged rooms, gray skinned Selina
measures out, uncurls gold leaf
where large eyed giants look beyond their
Byzantine glory blazing under a New York light bulb,

White witches hair brushing her waist,
with deep ringed eyes,
using coarse paint for potions
she makes her flat people like playing cards
give way to round pigs, lone goats, new found familiars,
come after a world of black and white figures
shadow histories of a pair of brown eyed girls
whose alphabet limbs in sober city grew,
while Selina painted herself
under firework skies, a Tai chi dancer
unreeling time as gesture.

We are bones, Selina,
even as our fat separates and turns to shit,
even as we walk the streets, grown thinner
and more delicate under our bear and bird coats;
your studio full with rockets and new suns blooming,
your animal heaven, our skeletal glory
proving only you are color-mad —
you and I, Selina, hands on flesh, painting away.

SCULPTURES BY THE TALL WOMAN

For Ursula von Rydingsvaard

Do these have something to do with being tall,
with being a tree of a woman with eyes that see far,
for whom mourning means examining a space
where shadows dig into wood and building
is a way of dealing with death? Cut, piece
together, connect man, woman, bird
into one large rough shape, into a dream of
standing in space — ritual, ritual
standing in rows, organizing hills
reaching that middle place. Now,
being a tree of a woman with eyes that see far,
you celebrate memory with wood bevels
like the ocean, shoveled from the brain—
like the mark, the groove, the print of a thumb
in wood to uncover a past.
The body is a stance learned on dark winter mornings
moving from place to place — *Kyrie, kyrie elision* —
living in barrack houses, going to barrack churches—
in landscapes of dark forests, armadas of birds
in the green grass. But memory is a liar;
Can a tree woman have ever been a child?
Your stride, these ghost patterns, memories
of husbands, fathers are altars for which
the laying on of hands is a litany.
Stand now, "touch wood, be safe and free,"
a child's game grown serious,
wood from the forest, space to become
hymned and loved
revealing how they went and died,
long, long shadows watching.

AFTER THE WARS

Re: The German painter Anselm Kiefer

You paint, you live where color is swallowed
by browns, gray, and umber,
where perspective stars in deep spaces
and calls *Sieg Heil!* to black forests
and burned landscapes
where gods are heroes
Das land, das land, covered with sand
abutting painted fires rising to the sky
where railroad tracks
take us to the top of the world
to blackened buildings, stone memories
and the cavernous rooms of the heart
where old lady history laughs back at
Germany, Germany, land where my cousins died —
Under acrylic, charcoal and shellac,
the gray and black of old newspapers
with maybe *der fuhrer's* photographs —
Das land, das land, lead covering over
the reality of photographs, instituting
a life of surfaces with "stories fit only
for women and children"
victims of straw into gold
writings on walls and canvases,
tree, and palette, Midgard, the giant serpent
in half light where covering over equals uncovering,
painting stands for belief and, you say,
in attempting to become a fascist,
you expand the boundaries of art
and understand whose madness?
The same marching, plunging into brown and tan

("only the French use a range of color")
the Shulamite is ashen, you say,
and because you are our murderers,
you are half of us, you say,
weaving straw into golden hair
in your pictures, with Horus and Osiris
and the blood of many Jerusalems
in your pictures.

ROWING AROUND THE CLOCK OF OUR HEARTS

Joan's poem

Oh, but I was fair with the sun a tondo,
beams and motes, accretions fine and delicate,
slim shadows slipping over the edge of the earth.

Today, in the studio, my eyes on a space walk,
I measure light as the sun rises
and deal with its mysteries, sun tints,
as my body under pulsing color becomes an enemy
and, with delicate insights, fights the reds,
rosy red risings of the blood pressure wars.

The glass tips mapping the wind and warm shades
of green and brown join
with everyday everything to be done over
but work is always worth working for.

Erase, scumble, restore, make perfect.
Rousseau's soccer players leave the ground
chase round and around after a shining ball
that makes the heart float and grasses grow
under my hand with hope at the top.

A note at the corner of my eye discovers
sands are the boundaries of seas,
triangles rise in a universe of stars and
vision will equal touch as I paint the mark,
the mark, the mark here in a rowboat of strokes,
a glimpse that reflects, gives back, and moves on.

CODA: MYTHOLOGIES

ISIS PRAYER

> After she married Osiris, he disappeared and Isis
> ruled Egypt in his place for twenty-eight years and then
> went seeking his body. She gathered up the fourteen
> pieces from fourteen cites, and put them together and
> Osiris became king of the underworld.

"I am dying, Egypt, dying,"
a world balanced on my hair,
surrounded by stone on stone,
surveying pyramids of steps steadfast
under the biting sands.
I, Isis, arbiter of female magic,
eyes rimmed black for that knowing look
the long stare — artifice the first law
by which bareness is achieved —
lie in an oblong box,
in a box within a box
a painted sky canopy protecting,
keeping my memories whole.
I, Isis, always smaller than you
among the armies of statues,
the rows of dulled sphinxes
ask who can you save,
what can you save — a laugh, a look
as the wind shifts, the sands move?
Seeking you in parts,
seeking you whole embraced by square stone,
your words on the wall across rows and rows of
pictures of spirits, of motionless flying birds,
Oh Osiris, my heart in the underworld,
swearing by the Book of the Dead

that addresses the living, swearing
"Not have I sinned, not have I done evil.
Not let be done to me anything therefore"
as I, too, swear here by the Nile
burying my feelings in underground searches,
a wife inventorying her history,
swears one day we will touch again
where the winds shift, the sands divide,
the water overflows as my heart overflows
and is met by sand.

RESCUE

If love were all, I'd fit him into
my box of minutes —
in this island which is
a handkerchief in the water
where a thread can be the key,
can be the world between my hands
as waves lapping, reach to where
Theseus, beside the labyrinth,
stands on my heart,
a victim like a god in the sunlight

who frowns, waiting on my brother,
the Minotaur, half bull, half man,
that Theseus sees as his rightful glory
even as I see in this prince
the beast's mirror image
who will change me and
change everything except
the sea in love's name.

As in love's name, Theseus
goes on to kill the beast and
I live the afterward,
covered in bull's blood
as he takes up and breaks Ariadne,
who held the thread to Knossus,

his face always turning into the wind,
offering a choice: The joy of being taken
or the tragedy of being left,

or the tragedy of being taken
and the joy of being left.

Glitter in the water, the sun under my hand,
"Always believe handsome boys' lies,
glittering tears now that the thread is gone,
now that love pulls you up and leaves you.
"Always believe handsome boys' lies"
the waves sing, sing, sun on the sea
and time on this island
to look around — time, time, time.

THE UNICORN OUTSIDE THE GARDEN

Inside a navy sky, the unicorn on the rug,
in the ring, on an island of *millefleurs*,
sits posing for history beside a tree.
Collared for love, the gentle head
holding aloft a horn of hope,
the silver striped lance like a small whale tooth
while a lady and a weasel,
"small in body but large in subtlety,"
music me as growing periwinkles press
against the wooden ring,
and burgeoning, burgeoning flowers
surround the unicorn, who rests on beds
of flowers. Innocent white center of the hunt,
emblem of improbability behind a pink fence,
a creature of misunderstood purpose,
Pegasus's son that none may ride stands
planted beside a tree. We dream him still
with that small beard. And what of
the lady with the bird on her finger,
while the unicorn poses as a heraldic figure?
Chivalry still the lady in the pen,
the unicorn on an island with the lady
with a gentle step puts a head in her lap,
seeing in a mirror, the hunt forgot, the hunt, the hunt!
The unicorn and she reappearing
surrounded by Gap khakis and "color me beautiful"
under a tent stuffed with bistort and English bluebells
on the red bed of the senses.
Scattered rabbits and hidden foxes
on the bed of picked flowers where
tame, tame the parakeet stands on her finger,

the unicorn sits at her knees.
Taste, touch, the hunt is past,
the unicorn is now in captivity.
Oh symbol of marriage, oh love,
collared and bleeding,
oh elegance without subtlety.
The unicorn is wounded inside a bed of navy sky,
is ringed, collared and bleeding;
the unicorn now in captivity
is wounded beside the pomegranate tree.

THE BEAUTY THING

I read about the beautiful dead model,
about how her world was not beautiful
except maybe for some minutes of seeing the moon
like an ice wafer beyond the mirror, her working space
that encapsulated the shining, beauty thing,
dark eyes and a full mouth, soul defining
like the tracks in my forehead, lined paths to my mouth,
defining us each in our skin envelope,
with no way to put out a hand and be what it isn't.

Some skin, some moon, the beautiful images
hit the big red drums of our hearts, stopping breath,
her fallen curl, we sigh, remote and so almost perfect.
And I read where she wanted to go beyond
the changing familiar, checking out her armor,
her ripeness which she regarded with exquisite, bitter pleasure
as needing to be lit, requiring proper shading,
expensive, expansive, love stopping at the surface,
coming off her best skin. See, how still young,
a prize photo of her shot nude behind a chain-link fence
smiling, the picture, a warning flash in her sentence
of drugged days piling up without direction,
her image, like a dare tacked up against her —
now gone, self-love nowhere to be found.

THE DETECTIVE

For John Henry

The detective of collapsed causeways,
wearing a red baseball jacket,
walks loose, scientifically;
a tracker, which means watcher
seeing the lover by the corner,
the strange girl praying in the subway,
a woman in mottled furs selling pins,
a sad dog, heels dug in, dragged along donkey style.
Between the detective's hands, real vanished hours,
strange weathers, someone playing music
in the south, while here in New York winter has come

with pieces of evidence of stars like opening hands
stars out of a book leading to another world,
even as I follow, circling the square
sunlight beaming on gray stone,
the time train inhaling static hours
while he signals tomorrow; pointing out
a skinny young old man with AIDS,
three buyers, ashen-faced in dark clothes.

"How's it hanging?" City scenery
at the end of the century
passing through a hundred nights
until someone finds her behind a door
which the detective maybe will break open
to what can't be reached or held,
changes in the falling light,
faces whirling through the club of sleep.

CERES or THAT WINTER

1.

In that tunnel of months,
there was no discovery, no recovery
and I couldn't see the sky
for crying for a word to be taken back
that would bring my daughter back.

Ceres roamed the earth
talking to fountains, asking after her daughter,
her grief reaching the heavens
which skittering birds crisscross
missing each other,
while I close my eyes, refusing
to believe in a dark prince
stabbing into muscle, into vein.

"The earth is the lord's,"
Ceres' earth, Ceres who is earth —
I read, wrapping myself in stories
learning how Ceres talks to water
as I grow into the twenty-first century,
where a phone rings in the middle of night
and a mechanized voice from a faraway place
like a hand rising up from a pool, asks
Do you want sex? Only to call back a day later,
the line clearer, asking "Would you like a fax?"

I want information, hating isolation
hating the fact of her body
quivering in an underworld of sleep —
Now how many veins has she left?

Ceres gained information by curing a sick child.
I get mine from PULP FICTION!
The jokes pile on while nine-year-olds sell needles
and sing to heroin, that glamour vamp,
what everybody knows and —
God, won't someone besides me see it's bleeding her?

2.

How to find what I can't find?
Persephone played beside a lake,
among beautiful girls to whom nothing happened
except for thinking how beautiful they weren't
with unblemished skins, running steps, shrieking whispers.

Why did they survive who never told
of seeing Persephone swallowed up,
her day lilies dropping to the ground?
As her mother and the earth turn cold,
the body sleeps and the mind weeps on
and I harvest the bitter crops of sadness
in city buildings whose long shadows
I used to think were shelters.

3.

Over the phone, long lines
of nothing carried on wires. Going down,
memory seeks in darkness for the once round face.
Were those poppy fields Persephone finally lay in?
I call and call, asking where she is sleeping:
Have you detained her? Who do I call now?

Ceres nurses someone else's child
and in that caring,

puts off the pain she walks with
while I only have the lost round face,
the lost voice along with the thought,
why should things grow,
why should the earth be green?

Try a lawyer as messenger?
Telephones and faxes race around the world
as news of her absence grows older.
I read how winged shoes went faster
than wires when all the world was an island.
Godless, I fly from place to place
with my love which I would wrap around her —
addict and daughter, separate categories.
Now I want to forget who she was under our sun,
yet remember before she entered that house
where she lives, remember
how Ceres wandered the earth mourning.
Now only in sleep is there the parade of her faces.

     4.

Awake, hold the world hostage,
pray to any god you find: *They don't find her.*
Zeus sits in tweeds, the head of social services,
detached, the busiest of gods, *They don't find her* —

We grow beyond touch, relying on machines
like fishing poles in space,
as Zeus weighs lives, informs the fates
who intervene to save whom he pleases

while his officers, in police blues,
look down from their desks —
at the ghost train riders

who, to the Olympians, are only cases,
only flickers of life over their working days
as they eat and chat over cigarettes
and the riders disappear into the cry of a half life.

READY TO WEAR

A neon sign high up in the sky
reads, "Protect me from what I want,"
and I feel suddenly watched because
that may or may not be true,
knowing further uptown
in scarfs like a cloud, girl goddesses
in stacked heels of cowboy boots,
wear three dimensional metaphors
even as weaving transforms the natural
and the artificial grows more beautiful
in a bright store, its stars, buying, buying —
Is that what I want: hushed models
breathing extravagance in shining mirrors
where their painted mouths float,
their hearts on furled sleeves
decorated in patterns of blazoned suns,
a consciousness feminine if not human
come here this day, this hour
in a dress to tell the times,
the sizes because what else matters
by the hearts of our watches?
God save our flock, including a passing girl
up to the neck in sequined dress
holding back the silent peacock's
shriek of pleasure, cawing to a friend,
abjuring love so final, like a run in her stocking,
a tear in her heart for this moment in a scarf,
safe in the moment, its watery pattern
able to hide anyone, standing apart,
enveloped and swallowed by the physical
that seems but never is simple.

ART MURDER

Come for me! I murdered a painting,
cut its heart out. I need the police.
Call the papers. Important:
cut out the whole figure
swinging in a chair,
cut up "Nude in Front of the Garden,"
the Picasso with the big P.
Call the papers!
Before I was more dead than she
hanging so quietly
looking back, double-faced
smiling, the body, girl body, mocking —
and mocking the painter, also mad
as he hung on the wall
that belly, breasts, and bush —
so pray for me, pray for me
following her black eyes.

Trust me to run free, knowing
I kill only the canvas of
a model who has no bones,
where I can hide, my head swelling,
I'm an Easter Island man gone begging
except for the knife. Sunday,
rising Sunday, beyond
the window frames, slats, or blinds,
secret locks for a mad man's mind,
see paint fingers, my knife edges
kiss the canvas to pay for
the losses of the lasso-like smile
indenting her cheeks, all he made,

what comes from the mouth
and comes from paintings are all lies.
And now that she is gone,
the tear, this canvas rag is mine
and, alone among green leaves,
I will sleep in his garden —
not Picasso, I the new Christ.

THE GREAT LADIES

Fly away ladies, fly away.
Emerge from your bloody menstrual bathrooms
in cinderella skirts
which achieve a ripple effect until
sought in the dark, dark ladies
be you ever so blond
fly away, fly away.

What will become of us,
what has become of us
and the pink and green flower
with the labial center
looking for heartbreak?
an old lady demands,
staring at our unsteady legs.
Is this now what becomes of great us
as we tiptoe around a lake of pain?

Fly away ladies, fly away.
Transform into butterflies
you so demure,
crown yourselves with leaves
and as great women pose
for history in profile
against the minutes
until your habits and makings,
your rejoicings,
until finally your children
fly away ladies, fly away.